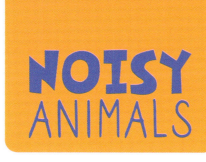

NOISY ANIMALS

Say "Good Morning!" at Home

By Madeline Tyler

www.littlebluehousebooks.com

Copyright © 2025 by Little Blue House, Mendota Heights, MN 55120. All rights reserved. No part of this book may be reproduced or utilized in any form or by any means without written permission from the publisher.

Little Blue House is distributed by North Star Editions: sales@northstareditions.com | 888-417-0195

Library of Congress Control Number: 2024936733

ISBN
979-8-89359-006-7 (hardcover)
979-8-89359-016-6 (paperback)
979-8-89359-036-4 (ebook pdf)
979-8-89359-026-5 (hosted ebook)

Printed in the United States of America
Mankato, MN
082024

Written by: Madeline Tyler

Edited by: Robin Twiddy

Designed by: Jasmine Pointer

QR by: Kelby Twyman

All facts, statistics, web addresses and URLs in this book were verified as valid and accurate at time of writing. No responsibility for any changes to external websites or references can be accepted by either the author or publisher.

Image & Sound credits
All images courtesy of Shutterstock.com. With thanks to Getty Images, Thinkstock Photo, and iStockphoto.

All sounds (s) by http://soundbible.com. Character – Lorelyn Medina . Front Cover – Vectors Bang, Sudowoodo, Maquiladora, NotionPic, Pogorelova Olga. 3 – Claud B. 4 – Mike Koenig (s). 5 – Armation. 6 – Miroslav Hlavko, Daniel Simon (s). 7 – Maquiladora. 8 – KAMONRAT. 9 – A7880S, NotionPic. 10 – satit_srihin, Mike Koenig (s). 11 – Vectors Bang. 12 – Natalia7. 13 – Maquiladora. 14 – fantom_rd, Cat Stevens (s). 15 – Maquiladora. 16 – Evgeniy Ayupov. 17 – Made by Marko. 18 – Vyaseleva Elena, Daniel Simion (s). 19 – Sudowoodo. 20 – Dr.Pixel. 21 – Vectors Bang. 22 – Rrraum, Daniel Simion (s). 23 – SunshineVector.

To use the QR codes in this book, a grown-up will need to set one of these apps as the default browser on the device you are using:

. Chrome
. Safari
. Firefox
. Ecosia

Your QR app might open the links in this book right away. If it doesn't, tap the button that says "open," "continue," "browse," or something similar.

We have lots of pets.
Our house can get
very noisy!

Scan the QR code to ring the doorbell and go inside.

4

Guinea pigs get lonely, so they like to live in pairs.

Scan the QR code to hear the guinea pigs say "good morning."

6

Pet snakes need to be kept in warm tanks so that they don't get too cold.

Goldfish live underwater. Can you see them swimming and splashing?

Say "good morning" and then scan the QR code.

10

Hamsters are full of energy and love to run. Exercise wheels are perfect for them!

This cat has a long tail that it uses to help it balance.

Scan the QR code to hear the cat say "good morning."

14

Chameleons eat insects. They catch them with their super-fast tongues.

All parakeets can sing,
and some can even learn to talk.

Scan the QR code to hear the parakeet sing "good morning."

18

Leopard geckos like to live alone and can live for up to 20 years.

Can you say "good morning" like a leopard gecko?

Dogs need exercise. They like to run, play, and go for walks with their owners.

Scan the QR code to hear the dog say "good morning."

22

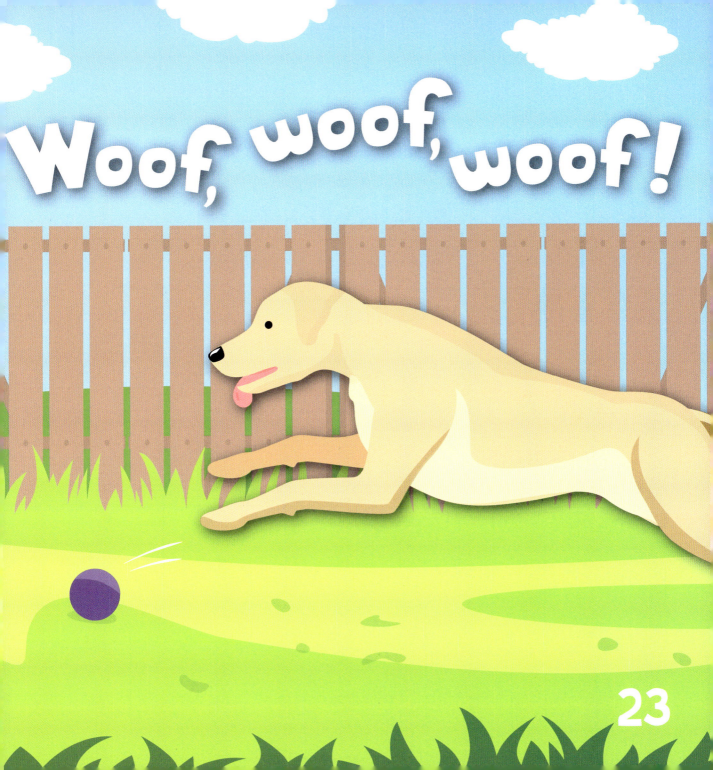